LIGHT IN AUGUST

NOTES

including
- *Life and Background*
- *The Circular Structure*
- *List of Characters*
- *Analysis and Commentary*
- *"The Individual and the Community"*
- *Notes on Main Characters*
- *The Lena Grove—Joe Christmas Correlation*
- *Faulkner's Style*
- *Review Questions and Essay Topics*
- *Selected Bibliography*

by
James L. Roberts, Ph.D.
Department of English
University of Nebraska

Cliffs Notes

INCORPORATED

LINCOLN, NEBRASKA   68501

Editor

Gary Carey, M.A.
University of Colorado

Consulting Editor

James L. Roberts, Ph.D.
Department of English
University of Nebraska

Cliffs Notes, Inc.   Lincoln, Nebraska

CONTENTS

Life and Background

Faulkner is considered one of the world's greatest novelists. In 1949, he was awarded the Nobel Prize for literature, which is the highest prize that can be awarded to a writer. In his acceptance speech, he said that the writer must be concerned with the human heart in conflict with itself. Certainly, the struggles of Joe Christmas to understand himself could be classified as the human heart in conflict.

Faulkner came from a rather distinguished Mississippi family. His grandfather, Colonel William Culbert Falkner (the "u" was added to Faulkner's name by mistake when his first novel was published, and Faulkner retained this spelling), came to Mississippi from South Carolina during the first part of the nineteenth century. The colonel appears in many of Faulkner's novels under the name of Colonel John Sartoris. And we learn in *Light in August* that Joanna Burden's grandfather and half brother were killed by Colonel Sartoris.

While *Light in August* is not Faulkner's most difficult novel to read, it is generally considered to be his most difficult one to understand. Various interpretations of the novels have been made, and, therefore, this guide offers only one of many ways of viewing this complex masterpiece.

William Faulkner was born in New Albany, Mississippi, but his family soon moved to Oxford, Mississippi. Almost all of his novels take place in and around Oxford, which he renames Jefferson, Mississippi. In his next novel, *Absalom, Absalom!*, Faulkner will include a map of this county and will show where many events in *Light in August* occurred.

Colonel William Falkner had a rather distinguished career as a soldier both in the Mexican War and in the Civil War. During the Civil War, Falkner's hot temper caused him to be demoted from full colonel to lieutenant colonel. After the war, Falkner was heavily involved in the trials of the reconstruction period. He killed several men during this time and became a rather notorious figure. (Thus the narration of Joanna Burden's grandfather's death at the hands of Colonel Sartoris has the ring of historical accuracy.) Colonel Falkner also built a railroad, ran for public office, and he was finally killed by one of his rivals. During all of these involved activities, he took time to write one of the nation's best sellers, *The White Rose of Memphis*, which appeared in 1880. He also wrote two other books but only his first was an outstanding success. The intervening members of the Falkner family are not quite so distinguished as was the great-grandfather.

In *Sartoris*, Faulkner's third novel, he placed his works in a mythological county. Most of the rest of his novels take place in this county. Thus, characters like Gavin Stevens, the farmer Armstid, and the Burdens appear in other novels dealing with Jefferson, the fictional county seat. One of Faulkner's great achievements is the creation of this imaginary county. He worked out this plan so carefully that a minor character in one novel — such as Gavin Stevens in this novel — will become a central character in a later work.

In all of his work, Faulkner used new techniques to express his views of man's position in the modern world. In his early works, Faulkner viewed with despair man's position in the universe. He saw man as a weak creature incapable of rising above his selfish needs. Later, Faulkner's view changed. In his more recent works, he sees man as potentially great, or in Faulkner's own words, man shall "not only endure; he will prevail." But in almost all of his novels, Faulkner penetrated deeply into the psychological motivations for man's actions and investigated man's dilemma in the modern world. Of his achievements, *Light in August* is considered one of the greatest, and in the character of Joe Christmas, many critics think that we have our only tragic figure in twentieth-century literature.

The Circular Structure

The structure of the novel is best seen in terms of a wheel or of a circular image. Actually, the central metaphor of the novel is also that of a circle.

Joe Christmas is the central character of the novel. His story is the hub or center of the novel, and the circular image is first applied to Joe as a cage which keeps him isolated from mankind. The earliest instance of his isolation is seen in his life in the orphanage. Later in life, he thinks of women, marriage, and children as additional ways to keep men caged in. He even cuts off all buttons — again the circular image — that women have sewed on his clothes. But the strongest symbol of his imprisonment in a cage is expressed through the conflicting white and black blood in his veins. Basically, the circular image is the principal image with Joe, as his life is presented in cyclic repetitions seen in the manner in which he constantly travels around the country until he finally arrives in Jefferson, Mississippi.

Although Joe has spent his entire life trying to break out of his circle, he finally realizes that he has lived only when he has remained within the circle. Thus, he attains peace through self-realization only when he reaches an acceptance of his life and no longer tries to flee from the responsibility of his actions. Joe, in other words comes finally to realize that his lifetime struggle was futile, since man can never escape from himself. The acceptance of this fact gives him the first peace of mind that he has ever had.

The circular image is used, therefore, to correlate the action with the structure. The central scene of the novel is Joanna Burden's house, and the cabin behind her house where Joe lives is described as the axle of a wheel where the numerous paths are like "wheel-spokes" caused by the Negro women "following paths which...radiated from the house." It is here at this place (the axle) where Joe murders Joanna Burden and it is also where Lena Grove later gives birth to her child.

The circular image, however, is first presented through Lena Grove. Her curving shape caused by her pregnancy suggests that she is "like something moving...without progress across an urn." The urn, then, is used symbolically in connection with Lena to suggest her enduring qualities. It is also one of the many symbols that connect life with death, since the urn is also used in burial rites.

Other images suggest the completeness with which Lena views life, and how she is fully immersed in a timeless world of natural surroundings. The final image of the first section is the circular column of smoke rising from Joanna Burden's house, which again connects Lena to Joe Christmas' actions. Lena, therefore, with her earthy nature, seems to represent those qualities which will endure forever; and the circular images connected with her (and with the action in general) suggests Ecclesiastes 1:4-6 "A generation goes, and a generation comes, but the earth remains forever. The sun rises and the sun goes down, and hastens to the place where it rises. The wind blows to the south, and goes round to the north; round and round goes the wind, and on its circuits the wind returns." Likewise, *Light in August* opens and closes with sections about Lena Grove.

Structurally, therefore, the circular image is used to suggest connections between Joe and Lena, to bring out certain qualities for which Lena stands and to act as an encompassing frame for the whole novel. She is the outside frame for the whole novel and the outside frame of the wheel (circle) transversing all experience and centering on no particular or specific experience.

Thus Joe's actions form the central part of the novel and are seen as the hub of the actions, but Lena's actions are used to introduce the novel and close the novel. In between these two stands the figure of the Reverend Gail Hightower. Whereas we meet Lena before we meet Joe, we also meet Hightower before we meet Joe. He is introduced immediately following the Lena (and Byron Bunch) section, and his section immediately precedes the closing scene of the novel. If then, the center or hub of the novel is the Joe Christmas section, Hightower stands between the center and the outside rim and connects the two. Thus, Hightower may be roughly compared to the spokes of the wheel, for through him the two strands of the novel are brought into a unity.

But then how does Hightower act as the spokes or connecting links between Lena and Joe? First the central metaphor connected with Hightower is that of the wheel. We see this image in the last part of the novel when Hightower begins to examine his life of isolation. As he reviews his life, his thinking "begins to slow" as though it were a "wheel beginning to run in sand." Hightower is then forced to re-examine all of his past life, which, for the first time, he is able to see objectively. As the wheel slowly frees itself from the sand, Hightower gradually realizes that life cannot be lived in isolation.

Hightower's involvement, however, was forced upon him. Byron Bunch involves him with Lena until finally it becomes his task to deliver Lena's child. Hightower then may be seen as the spokes, since he was forced to travel the same paths that Joe has traveled in order to help Lena with the birth of her child. Hightower returns from this place, which is Joe Christmas' house and the place where he had murdered Joanna Burden. And suddenly Joe Christmas escapes from the posse and flees for sanctuary into Hightower's house. Thus, Hightower comes from the birth of Lena's child only to be involved in the death of Joe Christmas.

Therefore, in terms of the total structure of the novel, Hightower is the spokes of the wheel connecting the actions of Lena and Joe, who never actually meet each other. Lena remains as the person transcending all experiences, and Joe is the character whose life is examined in depth in the center of the novel. The final structure then, may be summarized as follows: first, Lena (the rim of frame for the action); second, Hightower (the spokes of the wheel) and then Joe Christmas (the hub of the wheel). And the novel closes in exactly the same order—after we have completed the actions connected with Joe Christmas, the novel focuses again on Hightower and then closes with Lena. Thus briefly, the novel runs: Lena—Hightower—JOE CHRISTMAS —Hightower—Lena.

List of Characters

Joe Christmas

The central character, who in southern terminology, is a "white Negro" because he possesses a small amount of Negro blood.

Joanna Burden

An advocate for the Negro race who has lived in Jefferson as an outcast all her life. She befriends Joe and later becomes his mistress.

Lena Grove

A young girl who has walked from Alabama searching for the father of her unborn child. She is in her ninth month of pregnancy.

Byron Bunch

An employee in the local planing mill who reveals the whereabouts of Lena's seducer and then feels obliged to help her.

Reverend Gail Hightower

A minister who lives so far in the past that he can no longer enter into the stream of life in the modern world.

Bobbie Allen

A prostitute who befriends Joe when he is about eighteen even though she knew he was part Negro.

Simon McEachern

A righteous farmer who adopts Joe and then brutally beats him whenever Joe shows an independent spirit.

Mrs. McEachern

Joe's foster mother who tries to side with Joe, but is rejected by him.

Euphues ("Uncle Doc") Hines

Joe's maternal grandfather who places Joe in an orphanage and abandons him because he thinks Joe has some Negro blood. Later he demands Joe's death when he hears that Joe is captured.

Joe Brown, alias Lucas Burch

The man who fathered Lena's child and then left her. When he arrives in Jefferson, he changes his name from Lucas Burch to Joe Brown and lives in the cabin with Joe Christmas.

Percy Grimm

The brutal and self-righteous citizen who feels the need to mutilate Joe's body after he has already shot Joe.

Gavin Stevens

The District Attorney, who offers an explanation for Joe's behavior.

The Dietitian

The dietitian (Miss Atkins) is important because Joe's encounter with her affected his entire outlook on women.

Armstid

A farmer who takes Lena Grove home to stay overnight.

Martha Armstid

Armstid's self-reliant wife who donates her meager savings to help Lena Grove.

Analysis and Commentary

CHAPTER 1

During the course of the novel, Faulkner will investigate several varied themes connected with modern civilization. Some of the dominant ideas in the novel involve (1) man's isolation, (2) man's relationship to the community, and (3) man's inhumanity to man. Many of these ideas will appear to be negative or pessimistic when viewed from the standpoint of the main character, Joe Christmas. But by focusing on Lena Grove at the beginning, Faulkner is first giving us a brief positive view. While it is true that Lena is now isolated and alone on the road, she almost instinctively knows that people will help her even though, as with Mrs. Armstid, some of them don't approve of her. Also, she will evoke positive and favorable responses from the community and will receive help from many people. In contrast to the bitter harshness which Joe Christmas evokes, Lena inspires kindness and compassion.

Basically, Lena is presented as a simple and relatively uncomplicated person with apparently a great strength and determination. She never complains of her lot and never asks help from anyone even though she willingly accepts assistance. She possesses a simple and basic faith in life. Her responses to life are the fundamental reactions founded on the concept of charity and hope. She believes that she will be with the father of her child when it is born. She is always anxious to help those people who give her assistance, and she would always be obliged if others would share her meager meals with her. This will later be built into a contrast with Joe Christmas, who is unable to respond to people and who is seen to be constantly searching for food of some type. Likewise, the simplicity of Lena's approach to life will later be contrasted to Joe's complex approach to life.

The image of the circle is connected with Lena. First of all there is her curving shape owing to her pregnancy. Second, the urn images connected with Lena suggest her enduring qualities but the imagery is also used to connect Lena and Joe together by violent contrast. Because Joe saw urns as symbolic of the feminine, he rejected them as a type of death image. But in connection with Lena, the urn image suggests the endurance and eternity of life. This image will become clearer later as we examine it in connection with Joe Christmas.

Other circular images connected with Lena include various descriptions suggesting her eternal acceptance of life, the completeness with which she views life, and her complete immersion into her natural surroundings.

The last circular image is that of the column of smoke rising from Joanna Burden's house. This image again connects Lena with Joe Christmas. Lena is bringing life into the community at the same time that she sees the circular column of smoke which indicates that Joe Christmas has just murdered Joanna Burden Lena, therefore, with her earthy nature and circular images seems to suggest qualities which will endure forever.

CHAPTER 2

The reader should be aware of the time of this section. It is the day that Joanna Burden's house is burning down and therefore the thought of Christmas connected with Joanna Burden causes Byron to think about him; thus, the reader is introduced to Christmas long before actually meeting him.

Our first view of Joe Christmas is an objective one from Byron Bunch. He thinks that Christmas looks as though he belonged to no definite place in the world, no definite home or community. This description evokes the idea of the Christian symbolism connected with Joe Christmas. The reader should be aware of this aspect of the novel regardless of whether he accepts it or not. For example, Christmas' name is a derivation of Christ's name. We find out that Christmas has no definite home and belongs to the entire world. Christmas' appearance in Jefferson causes surprise, as did the appearance of Christ. Christmas arrived in Jefferson on a Friday, a significant day in Christian religion, and he was thirty-three years old, the same age as Christ when He was crucified. And like Christ, who had twelve disciples, Christmas has at least one in the person of Joe Brown. More significant analogies will appear in later chapters.

The reader should not feel that Faulkner is trying to retell the Christ story. But rather, by these various analogies to the Christ figure, he deepens Joe Christmas' internal struggle by suggesting as an analogy the depth of Christ's struggle.

Faulkner delights in playing or punning on names. Note that Lena thinks *Bunch* is actually *Burch* until she meets Byron. And the Bunch-Grove-Burch relationship is a rather lusty pun on that relationship.

In the preceding chapter, we saw that Lena gladly accepts food and willingly offers to share her own meager food with strangers; now we hear that when Byron Bunch once offered Joe Christmas something to eat, Christmas brutally rejected his kindness telling him to keep his "muck." This reaction offers another basic contrast between Joe and Lena. We also learn that in contrast to Lena, who seems to blend in with her natural surroundings, Christmas emphasizes the difference between himself and the world he lives in. However, we see a relationship between Lena and Joe in that Joe Brown (Lucas Burch) is connected with both of them.

This second chapter mentions all the principal characters in the novel. And all of them seem to have an unusual relationship with the community. One of the motifs, or ideas, that will be developed is man's relationship to his community. And in this chapter, we see that all of the characters are in some way isolated from their community. For example, we hear that Christmas has nothing to do with his fellow workers. Brown is new to the town and does not seem to fit in. Even though Byron Bunch has lived in Jefferson for several years, no one knows anything about him except the old Reverend Hightower, who is also an outcast from the town. We hear of Miss Joanna Burden, whom the town has rejected because she is friendly with the Negroes. And Lena has just arrived pregnant and unmarried. Thus, Christmas, Brown, Bunch, Lena Grove, Hightower, and Joanna Burden are all mentioned in this chapter, and all are in some ways isolated figures, or at least outside the normal flow of the community.

Essential to the development of the novel is the manner in which Byron reveals that Lena's lover is in the town. The occasion of the fire which coincided with Lena's arrival into Jefferson also prompted Byron to talk more verbosely than is usual, and through his harmless gossip, he inadvertently reveals the whereabouts of Lucas Burch (alias Joe Brown). The fact that he does reveal this information aligns him with Lena and he then feels partly responsible for her welfare. In later chapters, his feelings of involvement ultimately cause him to try to involve Hightower.

CHAPTER 3

This chapter is concerned mainly with giving the background to Hightower's life. We hear these things not from Hightower but from the town. It will be the end of the novel before we hear Hightower's view of these events and then it will be only as he re-examines them in a search for the truth.

What is clear here is that Hightower is influenced by some event connected with his grandfather's being shot while riding a horse. This event makes him want to remain in Jefferson in spite of the indignations that he suffers. Furthermore, Hightower seems in some way partly responsible for his wife's death, but this full realization comes at the end of the novel.

Hightower's view is that all he wants is to be left alone. By this he means that he wants the town to let him live in peace and quiet. This is one way of denying life, or refusing to become a participant in life, thus becoming a type of vegetable instead of a human being.

This chapter also prepares us for Hightower's attempt to escape life by living for some event in the past. The past has such a strong hold upon him that we discover he used any method available to him in order to secure a position in Jefferson and furthermore, he has undergone the tremendous suffering so that he can remain in Jefferson. Only later will Hightower be able to live again in the present and accept his rightful role in society.

CHAPTER 4

Chapter 4 offers a good opportunity for studying Faulkner's narrative method. A technique often employed by Faulkner in this novel and others involves the use of indirection and circumlocution. In other words, Faulkner will often approach his subject from an oblique position and will withhold important information, creating an air of tension. If the reader will carefully examine the manner in which Faulkner gradually unfolds his story of the house burning and the relationship between Joe Christmas and Joanna Burden, he will then understand Faulkner's narrative approach to much of his fiction. The most important information is saved until the end of the chapter. First Byron tells of the house and the arrival of Lena and the manner in which he inadvertently revealed the identity of her lover. Gradually, we learn that Joe Christmas and Joe Brown lived behind Joanna's house and only later do we learn that Joe Christmas and Joanna had lived for about two years as man and wife.

The revelation that two unmarried people have lived together out of wedlock is shocking enough to a small southern town, but the final shock and the horror comes at the end of the chapter when Byron reveals that Joe Christmas has some Negro blood in him; therefore in southern terms, he is considered a "nigger." Thus the shock of Joe and Joanna living out of wedlock is replaced by the horrendous realization that a Negro man has slept with a white woman. In terms of southern mores, this is more horrible than any other possible sin. The murder, itself, will become less important than the sexual act, and will ultimately culminate in the horrible castration at the end of the novel.

When Hightower hears that Joe Christmas has part Negro blood, he says: "Poor man. Poor Mankind." It is as though he correlates the plight of Joe Christmas with that of all mankind.

This chapter offers the first hint that perhaps Hightower will be drawn back into life. This is hinted through Lena's inquiries as to whether Hightower is still minister enough to marry someone.

This chapter also shows Joe Brown and Joe Christmas in some type of business and personal relationship. This relationship is another connection between Joe Christmas and Lena Grove, since Joe Brown is involved with each.

CHAPTER 5

The reader should, first of all, be aware that this chapter represents a short jump back in time. The events take place on the night and day preceding the death of Joanna Burden. The idea that returns constantly to Joe's mind is the forthcoming act of murder.

Having established that this chapter precedes Joanna's death, we should then notice the elaborate and symbolic rituals preceding the actual murder. These preparations are to emphasize that the murder was not committed in cold blood. Many of Joe's actions in this chapter are comprehensible only in the light of later actions in the novel.

First comes Joe's realization that he has been tricked or fooled by Joanna because he had thought she was pregnant. But then he realizes that she had lied about her age and was actually several years older than she had told him. She becomes then the symbol of all the women in his life who have lied to him or who have tried to destroy his sense of peace and security. Only at a later point in the story do we realize that women have tried to bring elements of disorder into Joe's life and that he has constantly fought against the corrupting influence of women.

Joe's first symbolic act is that of removing his clothes, and by walking naked through tall wet grass, he seems to be undergoing some type of cleansing ritual. Next, we see him revealing his nudity to a passing car. The interplay of light and darkness on his body suggests the conflicting white and Negro blood in his body. Then, he tries to reject all of the emasculating influence of women by going to the barn and sleeping with the animals, thinking that even a female horse is a type of male. This again suggests that Joe is attempting to deny the female world.

Following a brief sleep, he becomes immersed in phallic images—the ladder, grass, lumber, icicles, and his own dark serge trousers set off by his white shirt. The cracked mirror in the cabin also reflects Joe's conflicts as he can see and come to terms with only half of his self. In the valley, he rests and goes through another cleansing episode as he shaves, this time using the water from the spring as the mirror, thereby severing connections with all man-made objects. His next act is to destroy the whiskey which had been his chief means of income in Jefferson society.

Joe's last act before the murder is to visit the two sections of the town. He goes first to the white section, which he rejects because he senses his isolation from it. He then goes to the Negro section, where he is rejected and where he realizes that his isolation is complete. He then makes his way back to the house where the murder is to take place. Thus, Joe makes elaborate preparations for the murder, an act that will sever him forever from any hope of becoming a meaningful part of society.

The entire scene is interspersed with numerous images of black and white; and through it all, Joe carries his razor, which he is tempted to use not in the white section he rejected, but in the Negro section, where he is rejected. And as a thematic refrain, the phrase, *"All I wanted was peace"* runs through the whole scene.

For persons looking for a Christian analogy, the entire scene rings with Christian symbols. The baptismal ritual, the struggle comparable to Christ's struggle before the crucifixion, the night in the barn (or manger) are all echoes of actions of Christ, but these should not be used to suggest that Christmas is the Christ-figure, but rather to deepen Christmas' struggle by suggesting as an analogy the depth of Christ's struggle before His crucifixion, thus intensifying Christmas' struggle.

CHAPTER 6

This chapter jumps back in time to the earliest period of Joe's life that he can remember. This chapter narrates the episode which affected Joe's entire outlook on life and thus became one of the most crucial episodes in Joe's life. First, it was there that Joe first learned that he might have Negro blood in him and the remainder of his life is an attempt to compensate for these two bloods. Here also he received his name "Christmas," since he was left at the orphanage on Christmas.

Mainly, however, this chapter establishes Joe's attitude toward women and toward his concept of an ordered existence. Slipping into a dietitian's room, he stole some toothpaste because it was a new experience and it tasted sweet. Having eaten too much and at the same time having to hide in the closet where the dietitian kept her clothes, Joe became sick while the dietitian was making love with the young doctor named Charley. When the dietitian discovered Joe's presence, she immediately called him a "nigger bastard," forcing Joe to correlate his actions with his Negro blood.

Joe, as a child of five, knew that he had done something wrong and expected to be punished for his offense. The dietitian, not realizing that Joe was too young to comprehend her promiscuity, lived in fear that Joe would tell on her; at the same time, Joe lived in a state of dreadful anticipation, expecting to be punished for his offense. Instead of being punished, he was offered a dollar, and he could not understand this contradictory act.

The suspense he was kept in was an exhausting experience which destroyed his sense of the order of things. The suspense is also correlated with the fact that he was abducted shortly afterward from the orphanage by Hines, the janitor, and upon his return, is adopted by Simon McEachern. This one episode, therefore, destroyed his peaceful order of existence, and henceforth, he always felt that women were destroyers of his ordered way of life. Thus, later, many of his violent actions against women stem from his resentment against the dietitian, who first introduced him to irrationality.

Joe's desire to eat toothpaste becomes central to his entire life. In many scenes during the novel, Joe is motivated by his hunger and by his desire for food. Later he both meets Bobbie Allen in a restaurant amid the odors of food and encounters Joanna Burden while he is stealing food in her kitchen. The toothpaste also functions as a vague symbol relating to Joe's sexual life. In the next chapter, when he first attempts sex with the young Negro girl, he vomits as though he is still vomiting from eating too much toothpaste.

This chapter presents the religious maniac in the form of Euphues Hines. Even though the reader is not aware of it at the present moment, Hines is actually Joe's grandfather. His language resembles that of an Old Testament prophet and he constantly sees himself as either God's messenger or as God Himself. His influence on Joe, however, is questionable because Joe's main conflict comes from his relationship with women.

CHAPTER 7

The first scene in this chapter is a brilliant capturing of the self-righteous, overly religious individual. Mr. McEachern is so intent that Joe learn his catechism that he becomes an almost inhuman monster. He loses all of his sense of pure Christian values in his desire to *force* the young boy to conform to his view of Christianity. The paradox is brought about by McEachern's indignation that Joe would lay the catechism on a stable floor because that is no place for the "the word of God." Apparently, McEachern has forgotten that Jesus was born in a stable.

Important in this scene is Joe's determination to keep his own individuality and his refusal to accept McEachern's religion. In terms of religious allegory, one could see this as Christ's refusal to accept a foreign religion.

Later when Joe kills Joanna because she wanted him to pray with her, we should remember how Joe was brutally forced to kneel and pray with McEachern. This episode turns his mind against any form of prayer and makes him antagonistic toward any person suggesting prayer.

Note that even though Joe is hungry, he refuses to accept the food that Mrs. McEachern brings him. This is again a manifestation of Joe's refusal to accept anything from a woman, because, as with the dietitian, he cannot understand a woman's motivation. But later he does eat the food ravenously. Thus one of the central images connected with Joe is that of his constant search and need for food.

In the scene with the young Negro girl, notice that Joe is fully aware of the strong odors of the barn. He is again reminded of the sickness caused by the toothpaste which belonged to the dietitian and begins to feel sick from the odors and from the idea of sex. Thus, we begin to see that Joe's entire approach to sex is affected by his eariler conflict with the dietitian.

Later when he thinks of the whipping he will receive, he knows when he transgresses McEachern's rules that he will be punished. But this punishment fits into Joe's concept of order. Joe knows that he can depend upon a man, but women are unpredictable. This is again why he detests the interference of Mrs. McEachern. She, like the dietitian, represents a threat to his settled order of existence. Mrs. McEachern has, however, always tried to be nice to Joe, but because of the dietitian, he distrusts all women.

If one wishes to develop the Christian symbolism, one should observe the foot-washing episode that is narrated in this chapter.

CHAPTER 8

This chapter moves back somewhat in time. The last chapter involved McEachern's discovery of the suit. In this chapter, Joe recalls the events leading up to his buying the suit, that is, his meeting and affair with Bobbie Allen.

Joe was attracted to Bobbie because she had a small, hard, almost mannish figure. This emphasizes his repulsion to the "soft kindness" connected with women and his rejection of exceptionally effeminate women. Later, we will see that Joanna Burden also has a certain mannish quality about her.

As with many of the women Joe sleeps with, Bobbie Allen is associated with odors of food and cooking. Again, there are strong sensory images connected with Joe's encounter with women, emphasizing the influence of his initial encounter with the dietitian.

The reader should remember that when Joe was hiding from the dietitian it was partly the odor of her garments that made him vomit. And thus, when someone tries to explain to Joe about the monthly periods of the woman, he becomes sick again.

When Bobbie later offers an explanation, Joe must flee to the woods, where he vomits. As he is sick, he sees images of *urns*, each with a crack in it, emitting "something liquid, death-colored, and foul." This is the female image, and this image will later be developed into Joe's death image. The urn is also used for Lena, but for her it is symbolic of eternal life.

The affair that Joe has with Bobbie represents his first open and honest affair with a woman. With her, he reveals all the innermost thoughts of his heart and offers her his complete and undeviating trust. His absolute trust in her will later be the source for his betrayal, but the reader should now note the simple, uncomplicated faith and trust that Joe places in Bobbie.

But when he discovers that she is a prostitute, he beats her violently. This act is not performed from some moral condemna- of prostitution, but because Joe's sense of order and rightness are upset. As he had expected punishment from the dietitian, now he expects Bobbie to be a more simple and honest person. The violence that accompanies his discovery is typical of Joe's reaction everytime something occurs which does not conform to his view of the order of things, culminating, of course, in his murdering Joanna Burden.

CHAPTER 9

Joe's bitter attack against McEachern represents all the hostility that he has felt for years and his youthful desire to protect the woman with whom he has been sleeping, especially when she has just been attacked by McEachern.

Most important in this chapter is Bobbie's sudden betrayal of Joe. She was the first woman to whom Joe freely opened his heart. Joe's youthful love for Bobbie existed on an idealistic plane because he was able to confess his Negro blood to her and be accepted by her as an individual. However, her betrayal of his love, which is accompanied by the taunts of "nigger bastard," implants the idea in his mind that owing to his blood he must remain the isolated being. Thus the episode with the dietitian and the interlude with Bobbie Allen convince Joe that he will never be able to have a trusting relationship with a woman.

Chapter 9 brings to a close all the narration involving Joe's early life. The two main types of influence are extreme rigidity and religious mania as seen in Hines and McEachern as opposed to the loose morality of the dietitian and Bobbie Allen. Joe's conflict is presented in the contrasting manner in which he violently attacks (and perhaps kills) McEachern, and is, in turn, violently beaten up as a result of Bobbie Allen's betrayal.

CHAPTER 10

The years between Joe's eighteenth year and the time when he appears in Jefferson are covered rather rapidly and we learn only that he has wandered about the country in ever widening circles. He is thirty-three when he appears in Jefferson, symbolically, the age of Christ when He was crucified.

Again, the reader should be aware of Joe's sense of the order of things. To each prostitute during his years on the road, he would confess that he was a Negro. The confession always brought one reaction. When this pattern of behavior is broken by the prostitute who did not care whether or not he was a Negro, his reactions are violent, and he beats her relentlessly, and he becomes sick afterward. Thus Joe's violent outburst comes from the unconscious desire to punish the dietitian who had first violated his pattern of order.

As with the dietitian, the Negro girl, and Bobbie Allen, Joe's first meeting with Joanna Burden is also amid sensory odors and connected with food. He is actually eating his stolen food when Joanna appears and tells him he will find sufficient amounts of food.

CHAPTER 11

Joe's basic desire to reject everything from women is revealed in his relationship with Joanna. That is, even though Joanna leaves him food, he still prefers to steal it. And even though he had already seduced her, he prefers to violate her anew each time. With these acts, Joe is asserting his masculinity. He is refusing to allow the woman to have any influence on his life. And each time he sleeps with Joanna, it is "as if he struggled physically with another man."

The reader should compare Joe's reaction to the food that Mrs. McEachern brought him to his reaction to the food left for him by Joanna. In both cases, he violently hurls the food away.

Joanna Burden's story of her ancestors places her in a position to help Joe. She has inherited the burden of the Negro race. Her willingness to accept a person at his own value should have prepared Joanna to accept Joe, and throughout this chapter, it appears that Joanna is accepting Joe for what he is.

At the end of the chapter, Joe says he doesn't know his parents but that one was part Negro. When Joanna inquires how Joe knows that he is part Negro, he tells her that he doesn't definitely know, but he has always assumed that he has Negro blood. The point is that Christmas *feels* himself to be a Negro, and he has lived his life with this assumption. His problem, then, involves his belief that he possesses two bloods, and therefore, his attempts to reconcile these two bloods or to find acceptance for both are crucial to his life.

CHAPTER 12

This is the central chapter of the novel, relating the events which were only hinted at in the first chapter when Lena Grove arrived in town and saw the column of smoke. Earlier, we knew that Christmas had killed Joanna Burden and the intervening chapters have given the motivations and background to the crime.

The first part of the chapter deals with the complete corruption of Joanna Burden. Her and Joe's relationship went through three distinct phases. The first was the seduction which we heard about in the last chapter, then came the wild "throes of nymphomania," and finally, the third phase was Joanna's attempt to change Joe.

During the second phase, Joanna, in the excitement of her sexual relationship with Joe would often cry "Negro! Negro!" emphasizing that she particularly enjoys being corrupted by someone with Negro blood. Thus, in spite of her heritage, which should have conditioned her to accept the Negro as equal, this cry suggests that again Joe is not being accepted as a person of equality. This in itself modifies his relationship with Joanna.

The crucial change comes during the third phase. The reader should remember that Joe always thought of women as being destructive to his sense of order. The dietitian, Bobbie Allen, and unknown prostitutes have forced him to distrust the influence of women who seem to violate his sense of an ordered life. For about two years, Joanna and Joe's relationship conformed to an ordered (though unorthodox) pattern, but when Joanna broke this pattern with her demands that Christmas take over her finances, go to a Negro school, and finally that he pray with her in order to be saved, he again reacted violently to this violation of his concept of an ordered existence. Prayer is particularly offensive to Joe because of his earlier childhood experience with Mr. McEachern when the elder man beat him unmercifully because of his refusal to recite the catechism.

Joe also views women as being capable of destroying his own individuality. He thinks in this chapter that it would be easy to give in to Joanna and live a life of security and ease. But then he thinks that if he did give in, he would be denying everything that he has stood for during his life. Consequently, when Joanna tries to force him to change, he must destroy her or else his own sense of security and isolation is violated, and he loses his own individuality. On the simple plot level, Joe kills Joanna in self-defense because she did attempt to kill Christmas and would have succeeded if the gun had not failed to fire. Thus, in one sense, Joe kills out of self-protection.

He could have run, but again, he has spent his life running and now he feels that he must take his stand and assert his own values even if it means killing the person who is trying to violate his order and peaceful existence.

CHAPTER 13

This chapter handles the town's reaction to the crime before we see, in the next chapter, Joe's own actions following his crime.

Hightower's reactions in this chapter are central to understanding his character. Notice that when Byron Bunch discusses Lena's fate with him, Hightower refuses to offer his house as a refuge for her. He feels that he has suffered too much in the past and does not want to become involved in life again. Then after Hightower hears about the sheriff's finding Joe's trail, he feels some identity with Joe and is afraid that he is being drawn back into the stream of life. Even the fact that he feels something other than indifference to the fate of another person indicates that he is becoming involved with life again.

But he doesn't want to become involved, and even though he resists, Hightower is slowly being drawn back into life. At the end of the chapter, he reminds Byron to engage a doctor for Lena and casually offers to help if there is anything he can do. Thus through Byron Bunch, himself a person isolated from the community, Hightower is being drawn back into the stream of life even though he resists it at every turn.

In this chapter, it becomes apparent that Byron is falling in love with Lena Grove. Hightower still has the perception and sensitivity to recognize this fact and knows that it will only bring sorrow to Byron. So he tells Byron to leave this town, which he calls "this terrible, terrible place." Hightower has firsthand information as to how cruel and terrible the town of Jefferson is, and he fears for both Byron and himself. He prefers his life alone and has seen Byron live a life isolated from other people. He therefore fears that Byron is opening himself to terrible anguish and pain by becoming involved with a woman who is not accepted by the town.

CHAPTER 14

Since Joe felt the need to kill Joanna out of a need to retain his individuality and since he could no longer run from his own self, it is now significant that after the murder, he makes no attempt to escape. He never leaves the surrounding countryside through which he wanders trying to come to terms with his conflict, and since his is an inner conflict, there is no need for Joe to leave the immediate neighborhood of his crime.

The murder occurred on Saturday, and on a Tuesday, Joe is seen in a Negro church cursing God. After this dramatic episode, Joe begins to come to terms with himself. Some critics have viewed this as the day of the Holy Week when Christ cleansed the temple. But in terms of Joe's conflict with his two bloods, this episode suggests that the black blood can no longer remain pacified and must express itself in violence. This is his last futile attempt to deny the existence of his black blood.

His acceptance of his black blood comes when he exchanges his shoes for the Negro's shoes. Basically, this is done so that the bloodhounds cannot trail him, but in accepting the shoes, he also seems to struggle no longer with himself. It is as though he spent all of his energy cursing God in the Negro church and now is ready to accept his heritage.

As soon as Joe accepts his black blood, he finds a sense of peace and contentment for the first time in his life. Joe came to the realization that in order to have peace, he must accept full responsibility for his own heritage and his own actions. It is now that he realizes he must return to society and face the consequences of his earlier acts. With this decision and with his acceptance of his responsibility, he then finds that long-sought-after peace and contentment. This is represented by his becoming unified with nature and his surroundings: He breathes deep and slow, becoming one with loneliness and quiet that has never known fury or despair.

Note that as soon as he comes to this recognition and this acceptance of self, he performs a symbolic cleansing ritual by shaving in the soft, cold, spring water. He even uses the Negro's shoes to sharpen his razor and prepares himself for his return to town in order to assume responsibility for his actions.

It is only when Joe comes to the realization that he can never escape from himself and therefore accepts his Negro heritage that he breathes quietly for the first time in his life. He also realizes that he is no longer hungry. It will be remembered that Joe has always been in search of food and his sudden recognition that he is no longer hungry becomes significant in terms of his earlier struggles against hunger. Symbolically, when he accepts his destiny, he becomes at peace with his tormenting hunger, and also he sleeps peacefully for the first time.

Notice the difference in Joe's actions before and after his acceptance of himself. In the scenes which immediately precede and follow Joe's self-realization, there are different responses to Joe. In the first scene, Joe approaches a Negro in order to ask him the day of the week. The Negro is terrified by Joe's appearance and flees in utter horror. Then comes the scene after Joe has accepted his responsibility, and he approaches another Negro who quite naturally and nonchalantly offers Joe a ride into Mottstown. During the ride, Joe feels that he has achieved an acceptance for himself, and he realizes that he is no longer tired or hungry.

CHAPTERS 15-16

Chapter 15 gives us an excellent presentation of a religious fanatic. By presenting him as the town sees him, Faulkner gives "Uncle Doc" Hines the quality of a freak, a fanatic, a vile type of segregationist, and a pathetic weakling.

Even though old Doc Hines is not identified in this chapter as Joe's grandfather, the reader should at least recognize him as the same man who worked in the orphanage for five years between twenty-five and thirty years ago. He was the one who stole Joe from the orphanage and who called the action of the dietitian "bitchery and abomination" — the same thing he mutters at the end of Chapter 15.

On a realistic level, old Doc Hines' hatred of Joe is a result of his general hatred of the Negro race. Thus this chapter goes into a long presentation of his unreasonable dislike for the Negro race and his absurd interference with the Negro church services. Therefore, old Doc Hines' desire for his grandson's death can be taken on one level as the desire of a typical fanatic for white supremacy. But his fanaticism also functions on another level. It becomes significant when applied to his own grandson because this emphasizes Christmas' isolation from society; he can never be accepted when his own grandfather rejects him.

When Hightower hears the news of Joe Christmas' arrest, he becomes terribly agitated and begins to cry. Hightower has remained alone and isolated so long, has lived without human contact and knowledge of his fellow man for so long that now, as he hears of the suffering of another person, his compassion is intense. He feels even by hearing the story that he is being drawn back into the difficulty and strain of everyday life.

He reminds Byron that he is an isolated figure and no longer a man of God because the town forced him. Thus, Hightower seems to be suggesting that he is not responsible for his present situation and that he is not therefore capable of helping another person. But in actuality, Hightower does not want to assume the responsibility connected with living a normal life again—he prefers his own isolation without responsibility.

Chapter 16 also presents Joe's birth and the death of his mother. But whether he actually has Negro blood is left undecided. It was thought that his father had Mexican blood, but old Doc Hines and the circus owner both assert that the father actually had Negro blood.

We also find out that it was the dietitian who found and gave Christmas his name. This is ironic, since later his episode with the dietitian formulated his actions throughout the rest of his life.

Again those looking for the religious symbolism could view old Doc Hines as the Godhead. If so, then his rejection of Christmas makes man the complete victim of a hostile force. This analogy carries through with God demanding, requiring, or allowing the death or sacrifice of Christ.

We must remember that part of Joe's conflict came from his desire to escape the emasculating influence of the woman. He had always felt that the woman had tried to destroy his individuality. Here then we see another woman, Mrs. Hines, attempting in some way to modify Joe's decision to face the responsibility of his own actions. Mrs. Hines' interference will become a motivating force in Joe's attempt to escape in a later chapter.

Hightower's refusal to help Mrs. Hines is not merely a refusal to utter the lie she requests, but more important, it is a refusal to become an active participant in the community and thus become involved in responsibility again. Thus, his impassioned refusal is his last futile but passionate effort to retain his isolation.

CHAPTERS 17-18

Earlier in his life, Hightower thought that he had won for himself the privilege of remaining uninvolved in life. But gradually, since the appearance of Lena, he has slowly been drifting back into the stream of life. His re-entry into life is seen through the agency of Byron. Even though in Chapter 16 he rejected Mrs. Hines' pleas to help Joe Christmas, he does allow himself to go out to help Lena with the birth of her child.

The act of giving life to Lena's child becomes symbolic of Hightower's restoration to life. Immediately after this act, he walks back to town thinking that he will be unable to sleep. This is still an unconscious resentment of being drawn back into the stream of life, even though the aid that he gave to Lena was voluntary. Thus, when Hightower does sleep peacefully, we can view this as being symbolic of Hightower's regeneration as a human being. This is also seen in the fact that he notices for the first time the peaceful serenity of the August morning. He even realizes his own reawakening when he recognizes that life and involvement are still possible. He views the birth as a good sign and as an omen of goodwill. Therefore, this act of involvement and responsibility has restored Hightower to the human race. Another connection between Lena and Joe is presented when Joe's grandmother aids Lena during childbirth. Lena even becomes confused as to the paternity of the child and begins to think that Joe Christmas is the child's father.

Chapter 18 acts as a type of comic interlude with Byron arranging for Lena to meet Brown. In the midst of a novel dealing with Joe Christmas' tragic plight, this chapter reminds us of the basic incongruity of mankind. It shows Byron's dedication and love for Lena and prepares us for his final action of following Lena. Yet the action is detached and comic partly because of Lena's dogged determination to follow Brown when he leaves, and also because of Byron's absurd behavior. In juxtaposition to the comic are the tragic implications at the end of the chapter when Byron hears that Christmas has been killed.

CHAPTER 19

This entire chapter is narrated from the viewpoint of the town. After the last chapter, in which Joe found a certain peace within himself, he then returns to the community and apparently allows himself to be captured. Since none of the action is from Joe's point of view, the reader must speculate about what caused him to make a break after he had apparently given himself up and decided to accept his punishment.

The first explanation is offered by Gavin Stevens, a new character who functions as a type of commentator on the action. This character, Gavin Stevens, will appear frequently in some of Faulkner's later novels, but what the reader should remember is that any new commentator can give only partial reasons and partial motivations for the actions. However, Stevens' view that Christmas' actions were a result of the conflicting elements in his blood is to a large degree the correct interpretation. But Stevens is closer to the truth when he speaks of the role played by Mrs. Hines and how she and her husband, old Doc Hines, set peaceful elements into conflict.

In the preceding chapter Joe had come to the realization that he could gain peace only in isolation and could never be accepted by the society as part white and part Negro. Joe no longer rebels against the conflicting elements in his blood until the arrival of old Doc Hines, and then the grandfather's wild rantings and ravings cause Joe to despair, especially since his own grandfather is the chief person demanding Joe's immediate death.

It has also been developed throughout the novel that women function as a type of destruction to Joe's sense of order. Thus, having accepted his destined place in life and having accepted his death, the visit of Mrs. Hines probably set warring elements into conflict again. We must assume that she told him of the Reverend Gail Hightower, since Joe did go there when he escaped from the sheriff. Through Mrs. Hines, Hightower's house functions as a type of haven for Joe where he can find some type of sanctuary from the influence of women.

Whether Joe knows of Hightower's past tragedy with women is not important, since Joe does feel drawn toward this man who has also suffered at the hands of the community. At Hightower's, Joe's failure to fire the pistol and his submitting to the horrible atrocity indicate that he accepts his death in Hightower's house as an escape from the destructive forces of the society and of women. It is as though Joe wills his own death in a sanctuary away from the influence of women.

Hightower's attempt to help Joe Christmas by saying that Joe was with him on the night of the murder represents Hightower's re-entry into life. Previously, he had rejected life and wished to live in total solitude. But he has just delivered Lena's baby that day and has seen how great life can be, even for an old man; thus, his attempt to save Joe is his recognition of his responsibility to life and is also his hope to help another isolated person (Joe) discover the same thing.

Even this close to the end of the novel, Faulkner introduces a new character in the person of Percy Grimm. In later years, Faulkner commented that he did not realize at the time that he was creating a little Nazi Hitler. But the manner in which Faulkner develops these secondary characters attests to his greatness. Grimm, as his name suggests, represents the horrible atrocities which man can commit against his fellow man.

But Grimm is also another person who stands outside the mainstream of the community. Even though he was able to get some men to follow him, no one seems to be as cruel as he. His enthusiasm for his perverted aims far exceeds any normal reaction. After his castration of Joe, one of the men with him becomes sick and vomits, suggesting that even the average man who condescends to follow Grimm cannot withstand the brutality of his final act.

CHAPTERS 20-21

As with the second part of the novel, Hightower's narration stands between the central story involving Joe Christmas and the outer frame story concerning Lena Grove.

By aiding with the birth of Lena's child and then by attempting to save Joe Christmas, Hightower has re-entered the stream of life. And even though Hightower failed Christmas, he has achieved a type of salvation for himself. He does not realize this until much later on in the evening when he begins to review his whole life. Never before had Hightower examined his own motivations. But suddenly the whole meaning of his life evolves in front of him.

The use of the wheel image re-emphasizes the essential structure of the novel. The novel itself is seen in terms of circular images, and it is through this wheel image that Hightower sees man cannot isolate himself from the faces surrounding the wheel. Man must become part of the community and must assume responsibility not only for his own actions but for the actions of his fellow man.

Until the final pages of the novel, Hightower can never bring into a complete unity the two divergent accounts of his grandfather's death. He delights in the account of his grandfather being shot from a horse while brandishing his sword during Van Dorn's cavalry raid, but in the more realistic account, he realizes that his grandfather was killed by a shotgun while stealing chickens, and moreover, probably killed by some frightened woman. This last account, given by Cinthy, the Negro slave, finally succeeds in becoming the realistic view as Hightower attains a more rational grasp of life.

In both the opening and closing chapters, Lena is seen on the road. The only difference is that in between these chapters, Lena has acquired a baby and Bryon Bunch.

Since the novel closes with the emphasis on Lena, the reader is gently led away from the horrifying tragedy of Joe Christmas, and the final emphasis is on the renewal and continuance of life in the person of Lena's baby.

The Individual and the Community:
Faulkner's "Light in August"*

by
JAMES L. ROBERTS

Light in August is probably Faulkner's most complex and difficult novel. Here he combined numerous themes on a large canvas where many aspects of life are vividly portrayed. The publication of this novel marked the end of Faulkner's greatest creative period — in four years he had published five substantial novels and numerous short stories.[1] *Light in August* is the culmination of this creative period and is the novel in which Faulkner combines many of his previous themes with newer insights into human nature. In *Sartoris, The Sound and the Fury,* and *As I Lay Dying,* Faulkner had examined the relationship of the individual to his family. In his next major novel, *Absalom, Absalom!,* Faulkner returned to the family as the point of departure for his story. In *Light in August,* the family as a unit is replaced by the community, which although not examined as the family is in other novels, serves as the point of departure.

The novel may be interpreted on many levels. It suggests such themes as man's isolation in the modern world, man's responsibility to the community, the sacrifice of Christ, the search-for-a-father, man's inhumanity to man, and the theme of denial and flight as opposed to passive acceptance and resignation.[2] Each of these can be adequately supported, but none seems to present the whole intent of the novel. Perhaps this is because the complexity of the novel yields to no single interpretation but seems to require a multiple approach.

*Reprinted from *Studies in American Literature,* ed. Waldo McNeir and Leo B. Levy, Humanities Series, No. 8 (Baton Rouge; Louisiana State University Press, 1960), pp. 132-53, 170-72, by permission of Louisiana State University Press.

The complex theme of man's need to live within himself while he recognizes his responsibility both to himself and to his fellow man will support such a multiple approach to *Light in August*. The reaction of the various characters to the community offers another basic approach to the novel. Phyllis Hirshleifer emphasizes the isolation of man in the novel,[3] while Cleanth Brooks sees in it man's relationship in the community.[4] These two views do not exclude each other. The isolation of each character only reinforces his struggle for status both with the community and with himself.

Light in August follows in the logical pattern set by Faulkner's two earlier novels, *The Sound and the Fury* and *As I Lay Dying*. The preceding novels dealt with man trying to find a meaningful relationship with the immediate family, and this one deals with man in relationship to the community and as an isolated being unable to communicate with his fellow man.

Cleanth Brooks writes that the community serves as "the field for man's actions and the norm by which his action is judged and regulated."[5] But the difficulty here is that we do not have a sufficient picture of the norm. It would be accurate to regard the community as a force which man tries to assail or avoid. And as Miss Hirshleifer writes: "The society through which Lena moves, the people who give her food, lodging, money and transportation because of her patient understanding modesty are, after all, the same people who crucify the Christmases whose evil arouses their own."[6] It is, therefore, the responses of the community to the individual that become significant. While Lena evokes responses for good, Joe Christmas seems to arouse their evil instincts, and Hightower arouses their suspicion.

But these responses are not seen, as Brooks suggests, from the view of the community, but through the effects they produce on the individual character. Thus the community reacts in varying ways, but none of these reactions could accurately be considered as the norm of behavior. And even though Lena is able to evoke responses for good from various people, she remains outside the community. Each character in the novel is seen as a lonely individual pitted against some force either within or outside himself. Lena, Byron Bunch, Hightower, Christmas, Joanna Burden, Joe Brown, Uncle Doc Hines, and even people like Percy Grimm and McEachern stand outside the community. This is further emphasized by the fact that both Lena and Christmas are orphans who have no family whom they can return to. The community is also used as the objective commentator on the action. We get the long-range view usually from the point-of-view of the community, but nowhere during any of the long views does the community make any definite moral evaluations.[7]

The isolation theme is carried over into the structure of the novel. The novel may be broken down into many groups of seemingly isolated vignettes. Each scene, however, is part of one large thematic mosaic, and none could be successfully removed without destroying the whole. Likewise, each isolated character in each isolated scene is viewed in the final analysis as a part of the structure of a unified whole. Thus the isolation of each character is supported by the structural device of presenting the action of the novel in groups of vignettes.

Lena wills her own isolation. Although she could have left her brother's home unmolested and by the front door, she chose to leave by the window which had played such a prominent part in her pregnancy. She never complains of her lot and never asks for help from anyone. However, she instinctively knows that people will help her; so she comes to accept their help at face value. Her simple faith in life is echoed by her belief that she ought to be with the father of her child when it is born: "I reckon the Lord will see to that." Her responses to life are the simple and basic reactions founded on a simple philosophy of charity and hope. She is always anxious to help those people who give her assistance, and she would always "be obliged" if others would share her meager meals with her. She constantly feels the need to commune and share her experience with others.

Even though she relies upon the kindness of strangers, her strength lies in the fact that she has assumed complete responsibility for her acts. She blames no person for her ment, and she acknowledges no outside hostile force against her. Lena, then, brings with her the potential salvation and redemption of Byron Bunch and Hightower by evoking from them responses for good and forcing them to become involved in responsibility.

Byron Bunch, during his seven years in Jefferson before Lena's arrival, had only one acquaintance, the Reverend Gail Hightower, who was an outcast completely isolated from the community. The community had never noticed Byron, except in a casual way to comment upon his idiosyncrasies, until he became involved with Lena. Merely by her passivity and her simple questions, Lena forces Byron to become involved. After revealing to her the identity of Joe Brown, Byron then feels responsible to her. This feeling of responsibility draws Bryon out of his lethargic existence and forces him into the stream of life. He in turn tries to involve Hightower, who struggles against Byron's interference. Hightower has lived too long in his isolated world of self-abnegation and denial to see that Byron must feel responsible for Lena. He cannot understand Byron's actions and interprets them as possessing some ulterior motive.

But Byron's actions are the outcome of more than thirty years of routine monotony and celibacy. Byron, like Lena, had willed his own isolation in Jefferson; however, with the appearance of Lena, he is forced to become involved in society. His potential redemption is that he is able to live outside himself and commune with another person; and even though this involvement was forced upon him, his strength and salvation lie in the fact that he willingly accepts the responsibility for his actions. Not only does he commit the necessary acts of preparing for Lena's child and acting as her protector, but also, he exceeds the demands made upon him when he follows after the fleeing Brown and confronts him even though he knows that he will be beaten. Thus Byron, after willing his own isolation, has involvement forced upon him which he willingly accepts.

Hightower's isolation is likewise somewhat self-imposed. Initially, the isolation derived from forces over which he had no control. His grandfather's ghost haunted his Calvinistic conscience until it forced him to marry a girl whom he did not love and subject her to his own ghosts. He is haunted by two conflicting views of his grandfather—that of the romantic cavalry officer galloping down the streets with drawn saber and that of the grandfather shot while stealing chickens, and furthermore, shot probably by some woman.[8]

The seminary he attended acted not as a sanctuary from his phantoms, as he hoped it would, but rather as a means of furthering his ends and preparing him for a call to Jefferson. At the seminary, he met his future wife, who wanted to escape from the tedium of her life there. At Jefferson, he confused God with his grandfather, galloping horses with salvation, and the cavalry with Calvary. His sermons then reflected his own confusion and, as he later realizes, did not bring to the congregation the messages of hope and forgiveness.

When his wife commits suicide as a result of Hightower's failure as a husband, the congregation then turns against Hightower. He then becomes the rejected and isolated minister. Therefore, part of his isolation is forced upon him, but in part it derives from his own inner failure to bring the past and present into a workable unity.[9]

Carl Benson writes: "Hightower shapes his own destiny by acts of will, and he is, therefore, morally accountable for his choice."[10] It seems, however, that Hightower's earlier life was shaped for him from forces of the past over which he had no control. These are the forces which ultimately cause him to be rejected by the Presbyterian congregation. It is only after his dismissal that Hightower wills his own destiny, and therefore becomes morally liable for it. His choice to stay in Jefferson despite persecution, disgrace, and physical violence results in his complete isolation. His moral responsibility derives from the sanctity of isolation away from the community. He thinks that because he suffered the disgrace and shame, the physical torment and pain, he has won the right to peace and solitude and the privilege of remaining uninvolved in life. He refuses to accept responsibility for his past faults because his suffering has atoned for his previous errors.

But with the entrance of Lena into Jefferson, Hightower is forcefully drawn into the stream of life again and realizes that the past has not been bought and paid for. Hightower, therefore, cannot become the effective moral reflector of the novel until he is able to come to terms both with himself and his fellow man, and until he assumes a place in society again and recognizes his responsibility to himself and his fellow man.

Lena, Byron, and Hightower all will their isolation. Joe Christmas' isolation is forced upon him early in his life by outside forces and attitudes. Part of his plight in life comes from the fact that he can never accept anything but partial responsibility for his acts and at the same time attempts to disclaim all responsibility for them. Just before killing Joanna, he thinks that *"Something is going to happen to me,"* which suggests that Christmas looks upon his violent actions as being compelled by exterior forces which relieve him of any personal responsibility. But then this only increases his predicament, because he *does* feel a partial responsibility for his actions. If, then, Christmas' life and attitudes are shaped by exterior forces, it is necessary, in order to understand his plight, to determine how much Christmas feels he should be held responsible for his acts.

Joe's earliest attitudes were formulated in the orphanage. It was here that he first discovered that he possessed Negro blood —a fact that in one way or another controlled or affected his every act throughout life. His remaining life was spent trying to bring these two irreconcilable opposites into a significant relationship. His unknown father bequeathed him his Negro blood, and this heritage, over which he had no control, is the strongest influence upon his life. At the orphanage he is first called "nigger." The blood cages him in, and the vigilance of Euphues Hines sets him apart from the rest of the orphans. He is unable to establish a meaningful relationship with any of the other children, and he senses his difference.

One experience at the orphanage, especially, has multiple consequences for Christmas. When he is discovered stealing the dietitian's toothpaste, he expects punishment and instead is bribed with more money than he knew existed. This experience becomes the determining factor in his attitude toward the order of existence, women, and sex throughout the rest of his life. Since he was kept in suspense for several days desiring punishment which never came, he was left confused as to the meaning of his act.

Therefore, during the rest of his life when the pattern or order of existence is broken, the result is usually disastrous. When he transgresses McEachern's rules he expects and receives punishment, which accords with his idea of the order of things. This is again why he detests the interference of Mrs. McEachern. She, like the dietitian, represents a threat to the settled order of human existence. Or else, with each prostitute during his years on the road, he would tell her that he was a Negro, which always brought one reaction. When this pattern is broken by the prostitute who did not care whether he was Negro or not, his reactions are violent and he beats her unmercifully.

Thus his violent outburst comes from the unconscious desire to punish the dietitian who had first violated his pattern of order. The same reaction is seen in his relationship with Joanna Burden. For about two years, their relationship conformed to an ordered (though unorthodox) pattern; but when Joanna broke this pattern with her demands that Christmas take over her finances, go to a Negro school, and finally that he pray with her in order to be saved, he again reacted violently to this violation of his concept of an ordered existence.

His basic hatred for women ultimately returns to this episode. The dietitian in violating his order of existence also attempted to destroy his individuality. Thus the effeminizing efforts of Mrs. McEachern to soften his relations with his foster father are rejected because if he yielded to them, he would face the possibility of losing the firm and ordered relation with McEachern. As long as he maintains this masculine relationship with McEachern, he feels that he retains his individuality.

And, finally, the childhood episode with the dietitian is reflected in his sex life. The toothpaste becomes the basic symbol. At the same time that it is a cleansing agent, it also serves as a phallic symbol. The result of the scene is his utter sickness caused by the "pinkwomansmelling obscurity behind the curtain" and the "listening . . . with astonished fatalism for what was about to happen to him." Each subsequent sex relation, therefore, brings a guilt feeling to Christmas. He associated sex with filth, sickness, violation of order, and the potential loss of individuality.

Likewise, it is significant that each of his subsequent encounters with sex is accompanied by strong sensory images. When he beats the young Negro girl, it is amid the strong odors of the barn and he is also reminded of the sickness caused by the toothpaste. Later, his first encounter with Bobbie Allen is in the restaurant where he goes to order food, and finally, he meets Joanna in her kitchen when he is stealing food from her. Each of these sensory occurrences recalls to him the scene with the dietitian and again threatens the loss of individuality and the breaking of an ordered existence.

Christmas' need for order is violated in turn by each of the women with whom he comes into contact. The lesson he learned early in life was that he could depend upon men, but women were forever unpredictable. It was the woman who always broke the pattern of order. First the dietitian, then Mrs. McEachern violated his concept of order, and then Bobbie Allen turned violently against him at the time when he most needed her. The last woman to break his order of existence was Joanna Burden, who paid for it with her life.

The women, then, serve as the destroyers of order. This is brought out mechanically by Faulkner by using the biblical concept of woman as being unclean. Their menstrual period breaks the order of their life and then comes to represent their unordered and unclean life. The first time he learned of their monthly occurrences, Christmas' reactions were violent and ended in a blood baptism — the blood being taken from a young sheep that he killed. But even then he rejected this knowledge so that when Bobbie Allen tried to explain the same thing to him, again his reactions were violent, this time ending with his vomiting. When he next sees Bobbie, he takes her with force and animal brutality. Again, he seems to be reacting against his initial introduction to sex through the dietitian, again asserting his masculinity by forcing order upon the woman.

Christmas' great need for order reverts basically to the two bloods in him which are in constant conflict. As stated previously, his blood is his own battleground. He can neither accept nor reject his mixture of blood, and neither can he bring these two elements into a workable solution. Christmas' plight results from his inability to secure a suitable position in society and he searches for a society that will accept both elements of his blood. Unable to find this, he isolates himself from all human society.

Christmas' youthful love for Bobbie Allen existed on an idealistic plane because he was able to confess his Negro blood to her and be accepted by her as an individual. However, her betrayal of his love accompanied by her taunts of "nigger bastard" and "clod-hopper" implants the idea in his mind that due to his blood he must remain the isolated being.

His search for peace, then, is a search for someone who could accept Joe Christmas as an individual despite his conflicting blood. When Joanna Burden asks Christmas how he knows he has Negro blood, he tells her that if he has no Negro blood, then he has "wasted a lot of time." He has spent his whole life and energy trying to reconcile these two bloods, and if he has no Negro blood then all the efforts of his life have been to no avail.[11]

Joanna Burden should have been the person who could have accepted Joe for what he was. By the time of their involvement, Christmas no longer seems to revolt against being called a Negro. But Joanna fails him. In being corrupted by him, she seems to enjoy the corruption even more by screaming "Negro! Negro!" as he makes love to her. At thirty-three, Joe has learned to accept this name-calling without the accompanying violent reactions; he is living in partial peace with himself, even though this peace has been found only in complete isolation.

He must reject all of mankind in order to find peace. This is seen when Byron offers Christmas food and the offer is rejected. Therefore, when Joanna offers him jobs, wants him to go to school, or tries to get him to pray, he feels that she is trying to destroy his isolation and peace. He is then forced to kill her or allow his own individuality, order, and peace to be destroyed by her. Faulkner conveys this on the story level simply by the fact that Joanna planned to kill Christmas and would have succeeded if the pistol had not failed her. Christmas is then forced to kill her in self-protection.

His life, his individuality, his peace, and his order would have been destroyed by Joanna had he yielded to her. And her death is accompanied by Christmas' refrain: *"all I wanted was peace."* But even at Joanna Burden's house, Joe could not attain his desired peace with himself because the warring elements of his blood compelled him to tell others that he was a Negro. At least, he confessed to Joanna and Brown. If, then, he could achieve peace only by isolating himself from people and by rejecting all responsibility toward society, he could never attain inner peace until he could accept himself and his own blood, both Negro and white.

Since Joanna was an overpowering threat to Joe's sense of peace and order, he realized that he must murder her or be destroyed by her. But the murder was not one in cold blood. The elaborate and symbolic rituals preceding the actual performance suggest that Joe is involved in a deep struggle with himself. The murder, instead of resolving his minor conflicts, severs him forever from any hope of becoming a meaningful part of society.

It is significant that he does not attempt to escape. He never leaves the vicinity of the crime. On the Tuesday after the Friday of the crime, he enters the Negro church and curses God. This is the height of his conflict.[12] The white blood can no longer remain pacified and must express itself in violence. It remains now for Joe to come to terms with the conflicting elements within himself, and this can be done only within the circle of his own self; consequently, there is no need for Joe to leave the immediate neighborhood of his crime.

When Joe exchanges his shoes for the Negro's brogans, he seems to accept his heritage for the first time in his life. And with his acceptance of his black blood, Joe Christmas finds peace for the first time in his life. Like Lena Grove, who always accepted her responsibility, Joe realizes now that in order to find peace, he must accept full responsibility for his heritage and actions. And again like Lena, when he accepts this responsibility, he finds peace and contentment, and he becomes unified with nature. Following this recognition and acceptance, he undergoes once more a symbolic cleansing ritual. This time using the Negro's shoes to sharpen his razor, Christmas prepares himself for his return to town in order to assume responsibility for his actions.

It is when Joe accepts his Negro heritage and recognizes that he can never escape from himself that he breathes quietly for the first time in his life and is suddenly hungry no longer. This recognition that he is no longer hungry becomes significant against the background of Joe's earlier life, which was filled with a constant struggle against hunger. That is, when he accepts himself, he symbolically becomes at peace with his tormenting hunger and also he sleeps peacefully for the first time.

With his acceptance of his responsibility and his recognition of his heritage, Joe can once more approach others. This is revealed by the scenes which immediately precede and follow Joe's self-realization. In the first scene, Joe approaches a Negro in order to ask him the day of the week, and his mere appearance creates astonishment and terror in the Negro's mind. He flees from Christmas in utter horror. But immediately after Joe has come to peace with himself, he approaches another Negro who quite naturally and nonchalantly offers him a ride to Mottstown.

Joe now has achieved an acceptance for himself, and he thinks that he will sleep, but then realizes that he needs no sleep and no food because he has found peace within himself. Thus Joe has traveled farther in the last seven days than in all the years of his life, because for the first time he has come to a complete recognition of his own life and sees that the true value or meaning of life is within his circle where he is able to achieve an understanding with himself.

Joe's plight in life, however, is not resolved. He could gain a partial truce with society by isolating himself from society; or else, he could attain a full acceptance of himself, but note that this was achieved while outside the community in complete isolation. Once he has recognized his responsibility, he must then return to the community. And once again in the community, he comes to the realization that he can never be accepted by society. The realization of his complete rejection is made more terrible by the wild rantings of his own grandfather, who demands his death.[13] Thus, if old Doc Hines must persecute his own grandson, Joe realizes that there can be peace for him only in death. His escape finally, however, seems to be not so much because of the fanaticism of old Doc Hines, but rather because of the quiet persuasion of Mrs. Hines. Her appearance at the jail was probably Joe's final proof of the woman's need to destroy his individuality.

Doc and Mrs. Hines then contribute to Joe's death, since they set peaceful elements into contention again. Consequently, his escape is an escape from woman and also a search for peace and order through death. It is, therefore, logical that after his escape he runs first to a Negro cabin and then to Hightower's house. Through Mrs. Hines, Hightower has become the symbol of hope and peace to Christmas, and in his search for peace through death, he chooses Hightower's house as his sanctuary in which he passively accepts his crucifixion. His failure to fire the pistol is symbolic of his acceptance of his crucifixion and death and of his recognition that he can find peace only in death.

The violent death and castration of Christmas at the hands of Percy Grimm implant in our memories the atrocities that man is capable of committing against his fellow man. Grimm becomes the extreme potential of all the community when society refuses to accept its responsibility to mankind. Or as Hightower uttered when he first heard about Christmas: "Poor man. Poor mankind." That is, Joe's death is not as much a tragedy for Joe as it is a tragedy for the society which would allow such a crime as

Grimm's to be perpetrated. In Grimm's act, therefore, we see the failure of man to attain recognition, sympathy, or communion among other men and society's failure to accept man in the abstract.

But Joe's death was not in vain. Through his death and through the birth of Lena's child, Hightower has attained salvation in life by arriving at a complete realization of his own responsibility. Earlier in life, Hightower thought that through suffering he had won for himself the privilege of remaining uninvolved in life. But with the appearance of Lena, he becomes once more drawn into the active stream of life. This participation was not voluntary but forced upon him in the first instance (delivering Lena's child), but after rejecting Mrs. Hines's pleas, his second act (attempting to save Joe's life) is entirely voluntary.

Originally the attraction of Hightower and Byron to each other depended upon both being isolated from the community; but as Byron becomes involved, he draws Hightower in also. Until after Lena gives birth, Hightower struggles to retain his isolation and advises Byron to do the same. But Byron's involvement is too deep. Hightower's struggle for isolation becomes more intense as he sees himself threatened with involvement, especially when he is asked by Byron and Mrs. Hines to lie for Joe Christmas' (and in Hightower's words, mankind's) benefit. His refusal is his last futile but passionate effort to retain his isolation.

But Hightower goes to the cabin and successfully delivers Lena's child.[14] This act of giving life to Lena's child becomes symbolic of Hightower's restoration to life. Immediately after the act, he walks back to town thinking that he won't be able to sleep, but he does sleep as peacefully as Lena's newborn child. He notices for the first time the peaceful serenity of the August morning, he becomes immersed in the miracle of life, and he realizes that "life comes to the old man yet." He views the birth as a sign of good fortune and an omen of goodwill. Therefore, this act of involvement and responsibility has restored Hightower to the human race.

This was Monday morning. Monday afternoon, Hightower is faced with his second act of involvement when Christmas flees to his house for sanctuary. This violence which Hightower must face is his payment for recognizing his responsibility in life. But having assisted in the birth of Lena's child and having recognized his involvement in life, he can no longer retract. Therefore, having acknowledged a partial responsibility, he must now perform his act of complete involvement in life by attempting to assume responsibility for Joe Christmas.

And even though Hightower fails Christmas, he has achieved salvation for himself. He does not realize this until later on in the evening when the whole meaning of his life evolves in front of him "with the slow implacability of a mediaeval torture instrument." And through this wheel image, he sees that man cannot isolate himself from the faces surrounding the wheel. Man must become a part of the community and must assume responsibility not only for his own actions but also for the actions of his fellow man.

Notes to "The Individual and the Community"

1. In addition to *Light in August* (1932), he had also published such outstanding novels as *Sartoris* (1929), *The Sound and the Fury* (1929), *As I Lay Dying* (1930), *Sanctuary* (1931), and the short stories collected in the volume *These Thirteen* (1931), which contain such stories as "A Rose for Emily," "Dry September," "That Evening Sun," "Red Leaves," and "A Justice."

2. Some of these themes have been developed by critics, especially man's isolation in the modern world by Irwin Howe, *William Faulkner: A Critical Study* (New York, 1951), pp. 148-51; man's responsibility to the community by Cleanth Brooks, "Notes on Faulkner's *Light in August*," *Harvard Advocate*, CXXXV (1951), 10-11, 27; the sacrifice of Christ by C. Hugh Holman, "The Unity of Faulkner's *Light in August*," *PMLA*, LXXXII (1958), 155-66; and man's inhumanity to man by Phyllis Hirshleifer, "As Whirlwinds in the South: An Analysis of *Light in August*," *Perspectives*, II (1949), 225-38.

3. "As Whirlwinds in the South...," pp. 225-38.

4. "Notes on Faulkner's *Light in August*," pp. 10-11, 27.

5. *Ibid.*, p. 11.

6. "As Whirlwinds in the South...," p. 230.

7. There may be one exception. When Percy Grimm kills Joe Christmas, the other members of the posse, who were coerced into following Grimm, become nauseated at Grimm's atrocity.

8. Until the final pages of the novel, Hightower can never bring into a complete unity the two divergent accounts of his grandfather being shot from a horse while brandishing his sword during Van Dorn's cavalry raid, and also in the more realistic account of his grandfather being killed by a shotgun while stealing chickens. The last account, given by Cinthy, the Negro slave, finally succeeds in becoming the realistic view as Hightower attains a more rational grasp of life.

9. Many of Hightower's characteristics may be viewed in Faulkner's earlier characterizations, especially in Horace Benbow in *Sanctuary* and Jason Compson III in *The Sound and the Fury*. Hightower's ineffectual attempts to save Joe Christmas may be aptly compared to Horace's equally ineffectual efforts to save Goodwin. His tendency to isolate himself and detach himself from the outer world may be noted in Jason Compson III.

10. "Thematic Design in *Light in August*," SAQ, LIII (1954), 544.

11. There is also the implication of a more religious interpretation that if Christmas has no Negro blood, then he can no longer be a part of God's chosen people. "The curse of the black race is God's curse. But the curse of the white race is the black man who will be forever God's chosen own because He once cursed Him."

12. Holman, "The Unity of... *Light in August*," p. 157, views this episode as "the day of the Holy Week on which Christ cleansed the temple."

13. On a religious level, Hines could possibly be viewed as the Godhead, and then his rejection of Christmas makes man the complete victim of hostile forces. This analogy would then intensify Christmas'

conflict, and his struggle becomes the struggle of all mankind against the hostile forces of the universe.

14. The destruction of the black and the survival of the white is interestingly pointed by the fact that Hightower delivers only two children, a black one who dies and the white one of Lena who survives.

Notes on Main Characters

JOE CHRISTMAS

Early in his life, Joe came to the conclusions that he had Negro blood in him even though he was able to pass for a white person. As he later acknowledged, he has spent his entire life trying to reconcile this fact and trying to find some society where he is accepted as a person and not as a mixed breed.

The earliest things he can remember are connected with his Negro blood, His stay in, and later abduction from, the orphanage was directly related to the fact that he possesses Negro blood. His encounter with the dietitian at the orphanage — an encounter that affected his entire life — is connected with the fact that he has Negro blood, since the dietitian calls him a "nigger bastard." His adoption by the McEacherns was rapidly transacted so that the orphanage would not have to acknowledge that they had been harboring a person with Negro blood. And during the course of the novel, each person to whom he confesses this fact later uses it in some way to try to force a change upon Joe or to wreak vengeance upon him.

Consequently, Joe's plight in life consists of his attempts to find a place where he could belong as an individual where it would not matter about his conflicting bloods. Thus, often during the novel, rather than facing his problem and solving his inner conflicts, Joe will frequently use violence against someone who tries to change him. He is then never able to discover his real self until after the murder of Joanna Burden.

While hiding from the posse, he realizes for the first time in his life that in order to find peace, he must first accept full responsibility for his heritage and his actions. As soon as he comes to this realization, he finds that he is at peace with himself.

He then accepts his fate and returns to Jefferson and prison. But once more, a woman (Mrs. Hines) comes to him and destroys his resolution. He must then escape from her and can do so only in death.

Thus instead of pleading guilty and accepting a life sentence in prison, Joe escapes and invites his own lynching. That he willingly accepts and desires death is seen by the fact that he makes no attempt to fire the pistol, but instead, passively accepts the death imposed upon him by the grim man, Percy Grimm. But Joe's murder is at the hands of a man, whereas his life was destroyed by the women who threatened his sense of order and his sense of individuality.

LENA GROVE

Lena Grove is presented as a simple, uncomplicated country person who has great strength and an abundance of determination. Her approach to life is quite simple. She never tries to deceive people about her marital status and willingly accepts help from other people and is not offended when someone morally disapproves of her behavior.

Her responses to life are the simple and basic reactions founded on a simple philosophy of charity and hope. She receives help and food from other people, but when she has something of her own to eat, she is always "obliged" if others would share her meager meal with her.

Lena possesses an earthy nature which allows her to respond to all events of life with a quiet relish and enjoyment. She seems to enjoy sitting and watching the countryside float by. She savors every bite of her simple can of sardines and in general she seems to represent those qualities which will endure forever.

She is furthermore used to open and close the novel, offering to us a positive ending after the terrible tragedy of Joe

Christmas. She is the outside frame for the entire novel and the outside frame of the wheel (circle) which traverses all experience and centers on no particular or special experience.

Her nature is one that allows her to commune with other people. Her desire to share her experience with others often leads her to confess her situation rather than being silent about it. And even though she will rely upon the kindness of strangers, her strength is that she blames no one for her predicament. She accepts complete responsibility for her acts. Lena, therefore, brings with her the potential salvation and redemption of Byron Bunch and the Reverend Gail Hightower by evoking from them responses for good and forcing them to become involved in responsibility.

GAIL HIGHTOWER

Early in his life, Hightower had used any means he could in order to be called to Jefferson, where his grandfather had been killed during the Civil War. After losing his church and being beaten, he continued to live in Jefferson even though he was no longer accepted by the community. He had thought that through suffering he had won for himself the privilege of remaining uninvolved in life. But with the appearance of Lena, he becomes once more drawn into the active stream of life. This participation was not voluntary but forced upon him in the first instance (delivering Lena's child), but after rejecting Mrs. Hines' pleas, his second act (attempting to save Joe's life) is entirely voluntary.

Originally the attraction of Hightower and Byron to each other depended upon both being isolated from the community; but as Byron becomes involved, he draws Hightower in also. Until after Lena gives birth, Hightower struggles to retain his isolation and advises Byron to do the same. Hightower's struggle for isolation becomes more intense as he sees himself threatened with involvement. He is later asked by Byron and Mrs. Hines to lie for Joe Christmas' (and in Hightower's words, mankind's) benefit. His refusal is his last futile but passionate effort to re-tain his isolation. He then orders Byron and the Hineses out of his house.

Hightower's desire for isolation is related to his desire to live in the past and his refusal to confront the problems of the present. He has a romantic notion that his life ended before he was born because the past was romantic and dashing while the present presents unsurmountable problems. Consequently, he is content to live in isolation, reading Tennyson and avoiding any contact with life.

But after being drawn partially into life by Lena and Byron and then by Joe, Hightower begins to review all of his past life. He then struggles with his inner self and finally attains complete self-realization of his place in the universe. He knows now that man must become a part of the community and must assume re-sponsibility not only for his own actions but also for the actions of his fellow man.

JOANNA BURDEN

Joanna Burden's father and grandfather had both been fanatic on the subject of freeing and helping the Negroes. Her grand-father and her half brother had been murdered in the course of trying to help the Negro race. Joanna, herself, was brought up with the idea that the "curse of the black race is God's curse. But the curse of the white race is the black man who will be for-ever God's chosen own because He once cursed Him."

When Joanna was very little, her father took her to show where the graves of her grandfather and her half brother were hidden. At the graveside, he admonished her to remember that her kin were killed not by a white man but by a curse, and that she has inherited that curse and that none can escape it. When Joanna asked her father if she couldn't escape it, he told her "Least of all, you." Therefore, Joanna was born and brought up with the idea that she must dedicate herself to raising the Negro up to a higher level. Until the appearance of Joe Christmas, Joanna had spent her life helping with Negro colleges, advising young Negroes, and contributing to various development funds.

Joanna should, therefore, have been the person who could have accepted Joe Christmas for what he was — as part Negro and part white. But she fails him. Having remained a virgin for over forty years, Joanna's initial response to sex was that of a fanatic. She enjoyed the corruption, and she even prayed to God to allow her to remain corrupted for a few more years. She even seems to enjoy the corruption even more by exclaiming "Negro! Negro!" as he makes love to her. Thus Joanna seems to enjoy the fact that Joe is a Negro and seems to make a distinction between his two bloods.

When she reached an age where she could no longer enjoy being corrupted, she began to resort to her forefather's religious fanaticism. She began to demand that Joe change his way of life. She offers him jobs, wants him to go to school, and tries to get him to pray. When he refuses, she decides that she must kill him. She would have succeeded if the old pistol had not refused to fire.

Thus, Joanna Burden stands as an ironic contrast to old Doc Hines. Both in their own way were fanatics over the subject of race. And both tried to kill Joe Christmas. But in terms of Joe Christmas, Joanna's attempt to destroy him was more dangerous because she tried to destroy his individuality.

BYRON BUNCH

Before the arrival of Lena Grove, Byron Bunch had lived in Jefferson for seven years. During these years, he had worked six days a week at the planing mill, working overtime on Saturday afternoons and keeping an accurate account of his own time. On Sunday, he was always in a country church many miles away leading the church choir. Thus Byron Bunch was essentially isolated from the community. His only acquaintance was the Reverend Gail Hightower, who was also an outcast completely isolated from the community.

The community had never noticed Byron except in a casual way to comment upon his idiosyncrasies until he became involved with Lena. Merely by her passivity and her simple questions, Lena forces Byron to become involved in life. After revealing to her the identity of Joe Brown, Byron then feels responsible for her. This feeling of responsibility draws Byron out of his lethargic existence and forces him into the stream of life. He in turn tries to involve Hightower, who struggles against Byron's interference. Hightower has lived *too* long in his isolation to see that Byron must feel responsible for Lena.

Byron's actions are the outcome of more than thirty years of routine monotony and celibacy. Although he has never done anything that is wrong, Byron has never really been committed to life. But with the appearance of Lena, he is forced to become involved in society. His potential redemption is that he is able to live outside himself and commune with another person; and even though this involvement was forced upon him, his strength and salvation lie in the fact that he willingly accepts the responsibility for his actions. Not only does he commit the necessary acts of preparing for Lena's child and acting as her protector, but also when he follows after the fleeing Brown and confronts him even though he knows that he will be beaten, he exceeds the demands made upon him. Thus Byron, after willing his own isolation earlier, has involvement forced upon him which he willingly accepts.

Thus, while Byron is not a strong or particularly admirable character, he does change from an isolated man living a vegetable life to a person now involved and committed to living.

The Lena Grove –
Joe Christmas Correlation

One of the main objections to this novel is that there seems to be no relationship between the stories of Lena Grove and the Joe Christmas tragedy. It is always pointed out that Lena and Joe never meet each other. However, they function in the novel as opposites and thus should never meet. But there are many connecting links between them.

The first link is the column of smoke coming from Joanna Burden's house. This smoke signaled Lena's arrival in Jefferson and Joe's departure, thus making it physically impossible for them to meet, especially since when Joe returns a captured prisoner, Lena is giving birth to her child. And the contrast between these two opposing entities carries throughout the novel. Malcolm Cowley's objection (Introduction to *The Portable Faulkner*) that the themes "have little relation to each other," or Irwin Howe's reservations (*William Faulkner, a Critical Study*) concerning the "troublesome problems of organization" and the "evident flaw" of "looseness" seem unwarranted. The images of the curve and circle are used in connection with both. With Lena these images imply an acceptance and unity with life, but with Joe they represent the society from which he is isolated and the cage in which he lives.

Joe has been in Jefferson for three years when Lena arrives at the end of this third year. However, she comes to terms with the town almost overnight, while Joe was never able to adjust himself. This is the result of basic differences in their character: Lena is talkative, Joe reticent; Lena is willing to share her food, Joe rejects all proffered food; Lena's isolation is self-imposed, Joe's isolation is imposed upon him; Lena is in a search of life, Joe is in flight from life; Lena never complains of life, Joe is in constant conflict with life; Lena brings life and affirmation to the community, Joe brings death and rejection to himself and the community; and finally, Lena finds her peace in life while Joe can find peace only in death.

Thus Joe and Lena can never encounter each other because they are almost diametrically opposed. But still, they bring about the resolution by performing their acts and involvement on the same ground. Again the circle of smoke first introduces them to each other. Then we find that Lena's lover is Christmas' partner. They are connected through Brown, who has lived with both, betrayed both, and caused both to take to the road. Lena goes to Christmas' cabin, the scene of Joanna's brutal death, to give birth and renewal to life.

It is here that Hightower goes directly from the birth of Lena's son to Joe's death. And, finally, Christmas' grandparents assist in giving birth to Lena's child, which Mrs. Hines confuses with Milly's child. This results ultimately in confusing Lena as to the paternity of her child so that she confuses Joe Brown with Joe Christmas.

Thus through life and death, Lena and Joe are symbolically joined together. Life is reaffirmed for Mankind through the birth of Lena's child, the death of Joe Christmas, and the resurrection of Hightower. The child then becomes the symbol of the future world which brings all people together, giving new life and hope to all.

Faulkner's Style

Faulkner's style in this novel is not the typical Faulknerian style. Usually, his style has a complexity and an involved sentence structure. But essentially, he uses a more straightforward narrative style here. But the main stylistic achievement lies in Faulkner's ability to capture the essential qualities of his characters through his style. He changes or modulates his style according to the character of subject matter about which he is writing.

Thus, the chapters handling Lena Grove are presented in the simplest prose and in rather straightforward narration. This type of style blends with Lena's personality, since she is seen as an uncomplex person with one single aim. Faulkner employs a lot of dialect in narrating Lena's section and this use of dialect seems to capture the earthy nature of Lena Grove.

But with Hightower the style varies. There is no use of dialect in the Hightower sections. Instead, in these chapters handling the Hightower narration and episodes, the style is the most complex, and by Chapter 20, in which Hightower examines his past life, the style changes to one of severe complexity and difficulty. This is because Hightower is going into a complex and difficult re-examination of his past life.

With Hightower, Faulkner also uses the technique of the "stream-of-consciousness." This is a technique whereby the author writes as though he is inside the mind of the characters. Since the ordinary person's mind jumps from one event to another, stream-of-consciousness tries to capture this phenomenon. Thus Hightower, in re-examining his past life, juxtaposes many events of the past into one timeless collection of events, and in his mind removes all time barriers so as to see his life in one clear moment. This is a difficult task and Faulkner employed a rather difficult and complex style in order to convey this difficulty.

With Joe Christmas, Faulkner again varied his style. In some of the transitional passages where Joe is in the process of returning back to the past, the style is extremely complex. For example, before he returns to the episode in the orphanage, the style is difficult: "Memory believes before knowing remembers. Believes longer than recollects, longer than knowing even wonders. Knows remembers believes a corridor...."

This complexity then suggests the difficulty of returning to the past through the memory. But once this transition back into the past is effected, the style becomes relatively simple. For example, the actual narration of Joe's affair with Bobbie Allen presents no special difficulties.

Thus part of Faulkner's greatness lies in his style and the way he is able to adjust this style to fit the subject under narration. The style will always shift in order to lend additional support to his subject matter.

Review Questions and Essay Topics

1. How does the dietitian affect Joe's life?

2. Describe Byron Bunch's role. Is he superfluous to the novel?

3. How does Joe Christmas change during the course of the novel?

4. How does Hightower change during the novel?

5. How might Uncle Doc Hines' fanaticism be interpreted symbolically?

6. In what way does Joe's grandmother contribute to his death?

7. How does Hightower function as a connecting link between Joe and Lena?

8. How does Joanna Burden fail Joe Christmas?

9. In what way was Joe's murder of Joanna partly justified?

10. How does Joe's Negro blood affect his life?

11. Relate man's responsibility to his community to his responsibility to self.

12. Each character is in some way isolated. Write a theme showing how his isolation influences his actions.

13. How is the tragedy of Joe Christmas a local or sectional problem? How is it elevated to a universal plane?

14. Develop Joe Christmas as a Christ figure, particularly as the Christ of the twentieth century.

15. Prove that Hightower is actually the main character of the novel.

16. Relate each character's isolation to that character's particular problem.

Selected Bibliography

BECK, WARREN. *Man in Motion: Faulkner's Trilogy.* Madison: University of Wisconsin, 1961. The chief value of this study is that it gives many of the prominent critical theories about the major novels.

BROOKS, CLEANTH. *William Faulkner: The Yoknapatawpha Novels.* Yale, 1963. One of the outstanding studies on Faulkner and has section at the back filled with many individual insights into individual problems.

CAMPBELL, HARRY M., and RUEL E. FOSTER. *William Faulkner.* Norman: University of Oklahoma Press, 1953. One of the earlier studies and useful as a basic guide from which other critics evolved their theories.

CULLEN, JOHN B., and FLOYD C. WATKINS. *Old Times in the Faulkner Country.* Chapel Hill: The University of North Carolina Press, 1961.

FAULKNER, WILLIAM. *Faulkner in the University,* ed. FREDERICK L. GWYNN and JOSEPH L. BLOTNER. Charlottesville: University of Virginia, 1959. A series of taped questions put to Faulkner by students at the University of Virginia along with Faulkner's answers.

HOFFMAN, FREDERICK, and OLGA VICKERY (eds.). *William Faulkner: Three Decades of Criticism.* East Lansing: Michigan State University Press, 1960. A collection of some of the best essays written on Faulkner. A very valuable reference book.

HOFFMAN, FREDERICK. *William Faulkner.* New York: Twayne Publishers, 1961. A basic introduction to Faulkner as a writer.

Howe, Irving. *William Faulkner, a Critical Study*. New York: Random House, 1952. A general interpretation that gives a broad view of Faulkner even though there is a deficiency of "in depth" criticism.

Malin, Irving. *William Faulkner, an Interpretation*. Stanford: Stanford University Press, 1957.

Millgate, Michael. *William Faulkner*. New York: Grove Press, 1961. A useful introduction particularly for the beginning student of Faulkner.

Miner, Ward L. *World of William Faulkner*. New York: Grove Press, 1959. A brief account of Faulkner's family and the Mississippi environment.

O'Connor, William Van. *Tangled Fire of William Faulkner*. Minneapolis: University of Minnesota Press, 1960. Contains many excellent chapters even though some chapters on some novels deal with a rather specific aspect of the novel.

Slatoff, Walter J. *Quest for Failure: A Study of William Faulker*. Ithaca, N.Y.: Cornell University Press, 1960.

Swiggart, Peter. *The Art of Faulkner's Novels*. Austin: University of Texas Press, 1962. One of the best studies of Faulkner's major novels, which discusses the greatness of Faulkner's art.

Thompson, Lawrence. *William Faulkner: An Introduction and Interpretation*. New York: Barnes and Noble, Inc., 1963. Perhaps the best short study yet to appear on Faulkner, which brings together many of the obvious critical views about Faulkner.

Vickery, Olga W. *Novels of William Faulkner*. Baton Rouge: Louisiana Press, 1959. Perhaps the finest book yet to appear on Faulkner. Mrs. Vickery handles most of Faulkner's fiction in depth.

WAGGONER, HYATT H. *William Faulkner: From Jefferson to the World*. Lexington: University of Kentucky Press, 1959.

Here's a Great Way to Study Shakespeare and Chaucer.

Cliffs Complete Study Editions

These easy-to-use volumes contain everything that a student or teacher needs for an individual classic. Each attractively illustrated volume includes abundant biographical, historical and literary background information. A descriptive bibliography provides guidance in the selection of additional reading.

The inviting three-column arrangement offers the maximum in convenience to the reader. Shakespeare's plays are presented in a full, authoritative text with modern spelling. Each line of Chaucer's original poetry is followed by a literal translation in simple current English. Adjacent to the complete text, there is a running commentary that gives clear supplementary discussion. Obscure words and allusions are keyed by line number and clarified opposite to where they occur.

Bilingual Book Series

"10 minutes a day"

"Learning a foreign language should be made easy so anyone can learn at his own pace. It should also be fun. Why not? That's what these books are all about!"

Kristine Kershul — author

Speak and understand a foreign language — in only 10 minutes a day!

Your Guides to Successful Test Preparation.

Cliffs Test Preparation Guides

Efficient preparation means better test scores. Go with the experts and use **Cliffs Test Preparation Guides**. They'll help you reach your goals because they're: • Complete • Concise • Functional • In-depth. They are focused on helping you know what to expect from each test. The test-taking techniques have been proven in classroom programs nationwide.

Recommended for individual use or as a part of formal test preparation programs.